CHECKERBOARD BIOGRAPHY LIBRARY

U.S. PRESIDENTS

The
United States Presidents

GEORGE H.W. BUSH

ABDO Publishing Company

Heidi M.D. Elston

Published by ABDO Publishing Company, 8000 West 78th Street, Edina, Minnesota 55439.
Copyright © 2009 by Abdo Consulting Group, Inc. International copyrights reserved in all
countries. No part of this book may be reproduced in any form without written permission from the
publisher. The Checkerboard Library™ is a trademark and logo of ABDO Publishing Company.

Printed in the United States of America, North Mankato, Minnesota.
012009
072011
Cover Photo: Getty Images
Interior Photos: AP Images pp. 16, 19; Corbis pp. 26, 29; George Bush Presidential Library and
     Museum pp. 5, 8, 9, 10, 11, 13, 14, 15, 17, 21, 23, 25, 27; iStockphoto p. 32
Editor: Megan M. Gunderson
Art Direction & Cover Design: Neil Klinepier
Interior Design: Jaime Martens

Library of Congress Cataloging-in-Publication Data

Elston, Heidi M. D., 1979-
  George H.W. Bush / Heidi M.D. Elston.
     p. cm. -- (The United States presidents)
  Includes bibliographical references and index.
  ISBN 978-1-60453-443-6
  1. Bush, George, 1924---Juvenile literature. 2. Presidents--United States--Biography--Juvenile
literature. 3. United States--Politics and government--1989-1993--Juvenile literature. I. Title.

E882.E47 2009
973.931092--dc22
  [B]
                         2008045385

CONTENTS

George H.W. Bush 4

Timeline 6

Did You Know? 7

Early Life 8

War Hero 10

Striking it Rich 12

Working in Politics 14

Vice President 16

Forty-first President 18

War in the Gulf 20

Restoring Order 22

Election Defeat 24

Home to Houston 26

A Leader Again 28

Office of the President 30

Presidents and Their Terms 34

Glossary 38

Web Sites 39

Index 40

GEORGE H.W. BUSH

George H.W. Bush has achieved much in his life. During **World War II**, he became the youngest pilot in the U.S. Navy. For his service, Bush received four medals.

After the war, Bush went to college. He graduated in less than three years. Bush then moved to Texas, where he succeeded in the oil business.

In the 1960s, Bush entered politics as a U.S. congressman. In the 1970s, he served as U.S. ambassador to the **United Nations (UN)**. He also became the U.S. **liaison** to Beijing, China. By 1976, Bush was director of the **Central Intelligence Agency (CIA)**.

In 1980, Bush ran for vice president under **Republican** Ronald Reagan. They won the election that year and were reelected in 1984.

Four years later, Bush was elected the forty-first U.S. president. As president, Bush helped reduce the number of nuclear weapons in the world. And, he earned praise for his leadership during the Persian Gulf War. Today, Bush remains a leader with charity organizations.

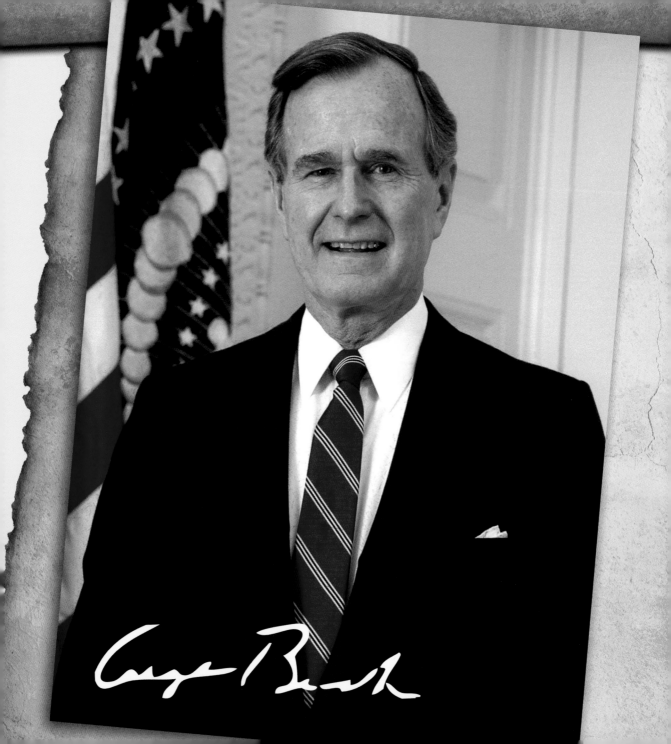

TIMELINE

1924 - On June 12, George Herbert Walker Bush was born in Milton, Massachusetts.

1942 - Bush joined the U.S. Navy on his eighteenth birthday.

1943 - On June 9, Bush became the navy's youngest pilot.

1945 - Bush married Barbara Pierce on January 6; in September, Bush left the navy.

1951 - Bush started the Bush-Overbey Oil Development Company with John Overbey.

1966 - Bush was elected to the U.S. House of Representatives.

1971 - President Richard Nixon appointed Bush U.S. ambassador to the United Nations.

1973 - Bush became chairman of the Republican National Committee.

1974 - Bush became the U.S. liaison to China.

1976 - Bush became director of the Central Intelligence Agency.

1981 - On January 20, Bush became vice president under Ronald Reagan.

1989 - Bush became the forty-first U.S. president on January 20; he handled the Exxon oil spill; in December, he led a military invasion of Panama.

1991 - Operation Desert Storm began on January 16; on February 28, a cease-fire went into effect; Bush and Soviet president Mikhail Gorbachev signed the Strategic Arms Reduction Treaty.

1992 - Bush dealt with riots in Los Angeles, California; he lost his bid for reelection.

1997 - On November 7, the George Bush Presidential Library and Museum opened in College Station, Texas.

2005 - Together with former president Bill Clinton, Bush raised funds for natural disaster victims.

DID YOU KNOW?

At Yale University, George H.W. Bush was accepted into the school's exclusive secret society called Skull and Bones. Each year, only 15 senior students are admitted. Over the years, many powerful individuals have been members. This includes U.S. presidents and U.S. Supreme Court justices.

Bush loved to play horseshoes. He even had a horseshoe pit built on the White House grounds.

Bush's oldest son, George W., became the forty-third president in 2001. Family members refer to Bush as "41" and George W. as "43." They are only the second father and son to be elected U.S. president.

EARLY LIFE

George Herbert Walker Bush was born on June 12, 1924, in Milton, Massachusetts. His family soon moved to Greenwich, Connecticut.

George's parents were Prescott Sheldon and Dorothy Walker Bush. George was the second of their five children. He had one sister and three brothers. Prescott and Dorothy raised their children to be well behaved and generous.

FAST FACTS

BORN - June 12, 1924
WIFE - Barbara Pierce (1925–)
CHILDREN - 6
POLITICAL PARTY - Republican
AGE AT INAUGURATION - 64
YEARS SERVED - 1989–1993
VICE PRESIDENT - Dan Quayle

Dorothy Walker and Prescott Sheldon Bush

Prescott served as George's model for public service. He was an investment banker and a moderator for Greenwich's town meetings. Prescott later served as a U.S. senator from 1952 to 1963.

Dorothy also strongly influenced young George. She taught him to be a team player. And, she stressed the importance of being humble and modest.

Growing up, George attended private schools. This included Greenwich Country Day School.

George with his sister, Nancy. George often shared his treats and snacks. Because of this, his family sometimes called him "Have Half."

In 1937, George entered Phillips Academy in Andover, Massachusetts. He was a serious and popular student. He was captain of the baseball and soccer teams. In his last year, he was elected class president. George graduated from Phillips Academy in 1942.

WAR HERO

In the navy, Bush flew an Avenger torpedo bomber. On it, he wrote the name Barbara.

America had entered **World War II** in 1941. Bush felt he needed to join the fight. So on his eighteenth birthday, he joined the U.S. Navy. Bush received flight training. Then on June 9, 1943, he became the youngest pilot in the navy.

Bush flew many dangerous missions during the war. On September 2, 1944, he was shot down over the Japanese island of Chichi Jima. For his bravery, Bush received the Distinguished Flying Cross medal.

Later that year, Bush returned to America. On January 6, 1945, he married Barbara Pierce. Barbara was from Rye, New York. The couple had met at a Christmas dance in 1941.

In September 1945, Bush left the navy. He then entered Yale University in New Haven, Connecticut. There, he studied **economics** and played baseball.

Barbara Bush

Bush graduated in 1948 and moved his family to Texas. There, he took a job with an oil equipment company called Dresser Industries. Bush learned the oil business quickly.

Meanwhile, the Bushes had started a family. Their son George Walker had been born in 1946. In 1950, Robin was born. Sadly, she would die three years later from **leukemia**.

Robin Bush

STRIKING IT RICH

In 1951, Bush and his friend John Overbey became business partners. They started the Bush-Overbey Oil Development Company in Midland, Texas. The company managed oil and natural gas properties.

In 1953, Bush cofounded the Zapata Petroleum Corporation. This company took over Bush-Overbey. One year later, Zapata formed the Zapata Off-Shore Company. Bush served as the new company's president from 1956 to 1964.

Meanwhile, the Bushes had four more children. John Ellis, known as Jeb, had been born in 1953. Neil had been born in 1955, followed by Marvin in 1956. Dorothy had been born in 1959.

By the 1960s, the oil business had made Bush wealthy. Yet, he was also becoming interested in politics. In 1964, he ran for the U.S. Senate but lost.

Two years later, Bush won a seat in the U.S. House of Representatives. He was the first **Republican** congressman to represent Houston, Texas. Bush was reelected in 1968.

The Bush family

In Congress, Bush supported some **liberal** laws. He was also named to the House Ways and Means Committee. No freshman congressman had been appointed to this committee in 63 years.

In 1970, Bush left the House to run for the U.S. Senate. Once again, he was defeated. Yet, his political career was not over.

WORKING IN POLITICS

In 1971, President Richard Nixon appointed Bush U.S. ambassador to the **UN**. Ambassador Bush worked closely with other countries. He served in this position until 1972.

During the Watergate scandal, Bush (right) remained supportive of President Nixon.

That year, the Watergate **scandal** erupted in Washington, D.C. On June 17, burglars broke into the **Democratic National Committee** headquarters. Some **Republicans** had hired them to steal secrets. They hoped the information would help President Nixon's reelection campaign.

In 1973, Bush became chairman of the **Republican National Committee**. As chairman, Bush led the Republican Party through this difficult time. President Nixon claimed he was not involved in the scandal. However, it soon became clear that he had played a part.

On August 7, 1974, Bush urged Nixon to resign. Two days later, Nixon left the White House. That day, Vice President Gerald Ford became president.

Ford then appointed Bush head of the U.S. **Liaison** Office in Beijing, China. In this position, Bush worked to strengthen U.S. relations with China. He served there until December 1975.

In 1976, Bush became director of the **CIA**. When **Democrat** Jimmy Carter became president in 1977, Bush resigned.

When Bush took over the CIA, Congress was investigating the agency's past activities. Bush worked to improve the agency's management.

VICE PRESIDENT

*President Reagan and
Vice President Bush*

In May 1979, Bush announced he was running for president. However, he lost the **Republican** Party's nomination to Ronald Reagan. Reagan then asked Bush to be his **running mate**.

On November 4, 1980, Reagan and Bush beat **Democrats** Jimmy Carter and Walter Mondale. Bush became vice president on January 20, 1981. Reagan and Bush were reelected in 1984.

Vice President Bush served as chairman of the National Security Council's "crisis-management team." He also headed several **task forces** on crime, **terrorism**, and drug **smuggling**. In addition, Bush traveled more than 1 million miles (1,600,000 km). He visited all 50 states and more than 60 countries.

In 1988, Americans had to elect a new president. **Republicans** chose Bush as their candidate. Bush picked Indiana senator Dan Quayle to be his **running mate**.

The **Democrats** nominated Massachusetts governor Michael Dukakis for president. His running mate was Texas senator Lloyd Bentsen. On November 8, 1988, Bush defeated Dukakis. Bush won 426 of the 538 electoral votes.

Bush called for a "kinder, gentler nation."

FORTY-FIRST PRESIDENT

Bush became the nation's forty-first president on January 20, 1989. In March, he handled the largest oil spill in U.S. history. Nearly 11 million gallons (42,000,000 L) of oil spilled into Prince William Sound, Alaska. Fishing waters were polluted, and much wildlife was destroyed.

Exxon Corporation was responsible for the spill. Many people were unhappy with the company's cleanup efforts. So, President Bush took action. He sent the military and other federal agencies to take over the cleanup.

Later in 1989, America had trouble with Panama. Panama's leader, Manuel Noriega, was involved in drug trafficking. In December, President Bush launched a military invasion of the country.

At first, Noriega escaped capture. Then on January 3, 1990, he gave himself up. U.S. soldiers brought Noriega to America to stand trial. He was sent to prison for his crimes.

During his election campaign Bush had pledged, "Read my lips: no new taxes." But, the federal government needed money. So in November 1990, Bush broke this famous campaign promise. He raised federal taxes.

Also that month, President Bush signed the Clean Air Act **Amendments** of 1990. The acts set tougher air quality standards.

Vice President Quayle and President Bush

WAR IN THE GULF

Bush was good at solving problems with other countries. As president, this helped him be a leader in world affairs. Bush showed strong leadership during the Persian Gulf War.

While Bush was president, Saddam Hussein was the leader of Iraq. Hussein claimed that Kuwait should be part of Iraq. So, Iraq invaded Kuwait on August 2, 1990.

World leaders tried to get Iraq to leave Kuwait. They feared Iraq would invade more Middle Eastern countries. But Hussein refused to withdraw his troops.

President Bush acted swiftly. He united other countries as **allies** against Iraq. And, he sent thousands of U.S. troops to protect Saudi Arabia from invasion. This military action is called Operation Desert Shield.

The United States and its allies demanded that Iraq leave Kuwait. Still, the Iraqis did not go. On January 16, 1991,

SUPREME COURT APPOINTMENTS

DAVID H. SOUTER - 1990
CLARENCE THOMAS - 1991

President Bush traveled to the Middle East to show his support for U.S. troops there.

America and its **allies** launched air attacks on Iraq. These attacks were named Operation Desert Storm. This was the beginning of the Persian Gulf War.

On February 24, the United States led a ground attack on Iraq. Four days later, a **cease-fire** went into effect. Bush told America, "It is a time of pride, pride in our troops, pride in the friends who stood with us in the crisis, pride in our nation."

RESTORING ORDER

Next, President Bush worked to improve relations with the Soviet Union. In 1991, he signed the Strategic Arms Reduction Treaty with Soviet president Mikhail Gorbachev. It reduced the number of nuclear weapons in both countries.

In 1992, President Bush faced problems at home. An African-American man named Rodney King had been beaten. The assault had been caught on camera and shown throughout the country. Four white police officers from Los Angeles, California, went to trial for the beating. No black citizens served on the jury.

The court did not convict the officers. This decision shocked many people and started **riots** in Los Angeles. Fifty-three people died. And, there was more than $1 billion in damage to property.

President Bush sent in troops and law enforcement officers to restore order. He also approved federal dollars to go to rebuilding damaged areas.

In December 1992, Bush again focused on helping foreign nations. He sent U.S. troops to Somalia. They assisted in giving food to thousands of starving citizens. The troops helped end the starvation.

PRESIDENT BUSH'S CABINET

JANUARY 20, 1989–
JANUARY 20, 1993

- **STATE** – James A. Baker III
- **TREASURY** – Nicholas F. Brady
- **ATTORNEY GENERAL** – Dick Thornburgh
    William P. Barr (from November 20, 1991)
- **INTERIOR** – Manuel Lujan Jr.
- **AGRICULTURE** – Clayton K. Yeutter
    Edward Madigan (from March 7, 1991)
- **COMMERCE** – Robert A. Mosbacher
- **LABOR** – Elizabeth H. Dole
- **DEFENSE** – Dick Cheney

- **HEALTH AND HUMAN SERVICES** – Louis W. Sullivan
- **HOUSING AND URBAN DEVELOPMENT** – Jack Kemp
- **TRANSPORTATION** – Samuel K. Skinner
    Andrew H. Card (from January 22, 1992)
- **ENERGY** – James D. Watkins
- **EDUCATION** – Lauro F. Cavazos Jr.
    Lamar Alexander (from March 14, 1991)
- **VETERANS AFFAIRS** –
    Edward J. Derwinski (from March 15, 1989)

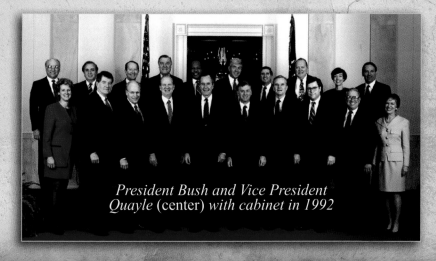

President Bush and Vice President Quayle (center) *with cabinet in 1992*

ELECTION DEFEAT

Meanwhile, the **Republican** Party had nominated Bush for reelection in August 1992. Once again, Vice President Quayle was his **running mate**. But the U.S. **economy** was weak, and jobs were hard to find. Many people blamed President Bush.

The **Democratic** Party nominated Arkansas governor Bill Clinton for president. Tennessee senator Al Gore was his running mate.

Texas billionaire Ross Perot ran as an **independent**. His running mate was former U.S. Navy vice admiral James B. Stockdale.

On November 3, 1992, Americans went to the polls. Many Republicans voted for Perot instead of Bush. Because of this, Clinton defeated Bush. Clinton won 43 percent of the **popular vote**. Bush received 37 percent, and Perot earned 19 percent.

Bush gracefully accepted defeat. He said, "The people have spoken. We respect the majesty of the democratic process."

Bush won just 138 electoral votes to Clinton's 370.

HOME TO HOUSTON

Bush with his sons George W. (center) *and Jeb*

On January 20, 1993, Bush and his wife returned to Houston, Texas. In retirement, Bush has maintained little involvement in the **Republican** Party. His biggest joy is spending time with his family.

Bush has had the pleasure of seeing two of his sons succeed in politics. In 1998, Jeb became governor of Florida. He was reelected in 2002. From 1995 to 2000, George W. was governor of Texas. In 2000, he was elected the forty-third U.S. president. He won reelection in 2004.

The George Bush Presidential Library and Museum opened on November 7, 1997. It is located on the Texas A&M University campus in College Station, Texas.

The library and museum is dedicated to preserving Bush's life and career. It contains photographs and documents such as personal papers. It also holds gifts Bush received while president.

The George Bush Presidential Library and Museum

A LEADER AGAIN

Twice in 2005, Bush helped with **disaster**-relief efforts. On December 26, 2004, a **tsunami** swept across several Asian and African countries. At least 225,000 people were killed. Some officials estimate the number is much higher. Millions of people were left homeless. Together, Bush and former president Clinton raised money to aid these victims.

In August 2005, **Hurricane** Katrina struck the southeastern United States. More than 1,800 people died. Thousands were left without shelter. Once again, Bush and Clinton teamed up to raise funds for the victims.

Bush has led a remarkable life. During **World War II**, he became the youngest U.S. Navy pilot. Bush went on to become a successful businessman.

Bush then served as a congressman, an ambassador, and vice president. As president, he showed strong leadership dealing with other countries. George H.W. Bush will be remembered for his many accomplishments.

Bush visited tsunami victims to express his sympathy to those suffering.
His involvement helped increase U.S. support for the victims.

OFFICE OF THE PRESIDENT

BRANCHES OF GOVERNMENT

The U.S. government is divided into three branches. They are the executive, legislative, and judicial branches. This division is called a separation of powers. Each branch has some power over the others. This is called a system of checks and balances.

EXECUTIVE BRANCH

The executive branch enforces laws. It is made up of the president, the vice president, and the president's cabinet. The president represents the United States around the world. He or she oversees relations with other countries and signs treaties. The president signs bills into law and appoints officials and federal judges. He or she also leads the military and manages government workers.

LEGISLATIVE BRANCH

The legislative branch makes laws, maintains the military, and regulates trade. It also has the power to declare war. This branch consists of the Senate and the House of Representatives. Together, these two houses make up Congress. Each state has two senators. A state's population determines the number of representatives it has.

JUDICIAL BRANCH

The judicial branch interprets laws. It consists of district courts, courts of appeals, and the Supreme Court. District courts try cases. If a person disagrees with a trial's outcome, he or she may appeal. If the courts of appeals support the ruling, a person may appeal to the Supreme Court. The Supreme Court also makes sure that laws follow the U.S. Constitution.

QUALIFICATIONS FOR OFFICE

To be president, a person must meet three requirements. A candidate must be at least 35 years old and a natural-born U.S. citizen. He or she must also have lived in the United States for at least 14 years.

ELECTORAL COLLEGE

The U.S. presidential election is an indirect election. Voters from each state choose electors to represent them in the Electoral College. The number of electors from each state is based on population. Each elector has one electoral vote. Electors are pledged to cast their vote for the candidate who receives the highest number of popular votes in their state. A candidate must receive the majority of Electoral College votes to win.

TERM OF OFFICE

Each president may be elected to two four-year terms. Sometimes, a president may only be elected once. This happens if he or she served more than two years of the previous president's term.

The presidential election is held on the Tuesday after the first Monday in November. The president is sworn in on January 20 of the following year. At that time, he or she takes the oath of office:

I do solemnly swear (or affirm) that I will faithfully execute the office of President of the United States, and will to the best of my ability, preserve, protect and defend the Constitution of the United States.

LINE OF SUCCESSION

The Presidential Succession Act of 1947 defines who becomes president if the president cannot serve. The vice president is first in the line of succession. Next are the Speaker of the House and the President Pro Tempore of the Senate. If none of these individuals is able to serve, the office falls to the president's cabinet members. They would take office in the order in which each department was created:

| Secretary of State |
| Secretary of the Treasury |
| Secretary of Defense |
| Attorney General |
| Secretary of the Interior |
| Secretary of Agriculture |
| Secretary of Commerce |
| Secretary of Labor |
| Secretary of Health and Human Services |
| Secretary of Housing and Urban Development |
| Secretary of Transportation |
| Secretary of Energy |
| Secretary of Education |
| Secretary of Veterans Affairs |
| Secretary of Homeland Security |

BENEFITS

- While in office, the president receives a salary of $400,000 each year. He or she lives in the White House and has 24-hour Secret Service protection.

- The president may travel on a Boeing 747 jet called Air Force One. The airplane can accommodate 70 passengers. It has kitchens, a dining room, sleeping areas, and a conference room. It also has fully equipped offices with the latest communications systems. Air Force One can fly halfway around the world before needing to refuel. It can even refuel in flight!

- If the president wishes to travel by car, he or she uses Cadillac One. Cadillac One is a Cadillac Deville. It has been modified with heavy armor and communications systems. The president takes Cadillac One along when visiting other countries if secure transportation will be needed.

- The president also travels on a helicopter called Marine One. Like the presidential car, Marine One accompanies the president when traveling abroad if necessary.

- Sometimes, the president needs to get away and relax with family and friends. Camp David is the official presidential retreat. It is located in the cool, wooded mountains in Maryland. The U.S. Navy maintains the retreat, and the U.S. Marine Corps keeps it secure. The camp offers swimming, tennis, golf, and hiking.

- When the president leaves office, he or she receives Secret Service protection for ten more years. He or she also receives a yearly pension of $191,300 and funding for office space, supplies, and staff.

PRESIDENTS AND THEIR TERMS

PRESIDENT	PARTY	TOOK OFFICE	LEFT OFFICE	TERMS SERVED	VICE PRESIDENT
George Washington	None	April 30, 1789	March 4, 1797	Two	John Adams
John Adams	Federalist	March 4, 1797	March 4, 1801	One	Thomas Jefferson
Thomas Jefferson	Democratic-Republican	March 4, 1801	March 4, 1809	Two	Aaron Burr, George Clinton
James Madison	Democratic-Republican	March 4, 1809	March 4, 1817	Two	George Clinton, Elbridge Gerry
James Monroe	Democratic-Republican	March 4, 1817	March 4, 1825	Two	Daniel D. Tompkins
John Quincy Adams	Democratic-Republican	March 4, 1825	March 4, 1829	One	John C. Calhoun
Andrew Jackson	Democrat	March 4, 1829	March 4, 1837	Two	John C. Calhoun, Martin Van Buren
Martin Van Buren	Democrat	March 4, 1837	March 4, 1841	One	Richard M. Johnson
William H. Harrison	Whig	March 4, 1841	April 4, 1841	Died During First Term	John Tyler
John Tyler	Whig	April 6, 1841	March 4, 1845	Completed Harrison's Term	Office Vacant
James K. Polk	Democrat	March 4, 1845	March 4, 1849	One	George M. Dallas
Zachary Taylor	Whig	March 5, 1849	July 9, 1850	Died During First Term	Millard Fillmore

PRESIDENT	PARTY	TOOK OFFICE	LEFT OFFICE	TERMS SERVED	VICE PRESIDENT
Millard Fillmore	Whig	July 10, 1850	March 4, 1853	Completed Taylor's Term	Office Vacant
Franklin Pierce	Democrat	March 4, 1853	March 4, 1857	One	William R.D. King
James Buchanan	Democrat	March 4, 1857	March 4, 1861	One	John C. Breckinridge
Abraham Lincoln	Republican	March 4, 1861	April 15, 1865	Served One Term, Died During Second Term	Hannibal Hamlin, Andrew Johnson
Andrew Johnson	Democrat	April 15, 1865	March 4, 1869	Completed Lincoln's Second Term	Office Vacant
Ulysses S. Grant	Republican	March 4, 1869	March 4, 1877	Two	Schuyler Colfax, Henry Wilson
Rutherford B. Hayes	Republican	March 3, 1877	March 4, 1881	One	William A. Wheeler
James A. Garfield	Republican	March 4, 1881	September 19, 1881	Died During First Term	Chester Arthur
Chester Arthur	Republican	September 20, 1881	March 4, 1885	Completed Garfield's Term	Office Vacant
Grover Cleveland	Democrat	March 4, 1885	March 4, 1889	One	Thomas A. Hendricks
Benjamin Harrison	Republican	March 4, 1889	March 4, 1893	One	Levi P. Morton
Grover Cleveland	Democrat	March 4, 1893	March 4, 1897	One	Adlai E. Stevenson
William McKinley	Republican	March 4, 1897	September 14, 1901	Served One Term, Died During Second Term	Garret A. Hobart, Theodore Roosevelt

PRESIDENT	PARTY	TOOK OFFICE	LEFT OFFICE	TERMS SERVED	VICE PRESIDENT
Theodore Roosevelt	Republican	September 14, 1901	March 4, 1909	Completed McKinley's Second Term, Served One Term	Office Vacant, Charles Fairbanks
William Taft	Republican	March 4, 1909	March 4, 1913	One	James S. Sherman
Woodrow Wilson	Democrat	March 4, 1913	March 4, 1921	Two	Thomas R. Marshall
Warren G. Harding	Republican	March 4, 1921	August 2, 1923	Died During First Term	Calvin Coolidge
Calvin Coolidge	Republican	August 3, 1923	March 4, 1929	Completed Harding's Term, Served One Term	Office Vacant, Charles Dawes
Herbert Hoover	Republican	March 4, 1929	March 4, 1933	One	Charles Curtis
Franklin D. Roosevelt	Democrat	March 4, 1933	April 12, 1945	Served Three Terms, Died During Fourth Term	John Nance Garner, Henry A. Wallace, Harry S. Truman
Harry S. Truman	Democrat	April 12, 1945	January 20, 1953	Completed Roosevelt's Fourth Term, Served One Term	Office Vacant, Alben Barkley
Dwight D. Eisenhower	Republican	January 20, 1953	January 20, 1961	Two	Richard Nixon
John F. Kennedy	Democrat	January 20, 1961	November 22, 1963	Died During First Term	Lyndon B. Johnson
Lyndon B. Johnson	Democrat	November 22, 1963	January 20, 1969	Completed Kennedy's Term, Served One Term	Office Vacant, Hubert H. Humphrey
Richard Nixon	Republican	January 20, 1969	August 9, 1974	Completed First Term, Resigned During Second Term	Spiro T. Agnew, Gerald Ford

PRESIDENTS 26–37, 1901–1974

PRESIDENT	PARTY	TOOK OFFICE	LEFT OFFICE	TERMS SERVED	VICE PRESIDENT
Gerald Ford	Republican	August 9, 1974	January 20, 1977	Completed Nixon's Second Term	Nelson A. Rockefeller
Jimmy Carter	Democrat	January 20, 1977	January 20, 1981	One	Walter Mondale
Ronald Reagan	Republican	January 20, 1981	January 20, 1989	Two	George H.W. Bush
George H.W. Bush	Republican	January 20, 1989	January 20, 1993	One	Dan Quayle
Bill Clinton	Democrat	January 20, 1993	January 20, 2001	Two	Al Gore
George W. Bush	Republican	January 20, 2001	January 20, 2009	Two	Dick Cheney
Barack Obama	Democrat	January 20, 2009			Joe Biden

"This is America . . . a brilliant diversity spread like stars, like a thousand points of light in a broad and peaceful sky."
George H.W. Bush

WRITE TO THE PRESIDENT

You may write to the president at:

The White House
1600 Pennsylvania Avenue NW
Washington, DC 20500

You may e-mail the president at:
comments@whitehouse.gov

GLOSSARY

ally - a person, a group, or a nation united with another for some special purpose.

amendment - a change made or offered in a law, a bill, or a motion by adding, removing, or altering language.

cease-fire - a suspension of hostile activities.

Central Intelligence Agency (CIA) - the U.S. government's main foreign intelligence and counterintelligence agency.

Democrat - a member of the Democratic political party. Democrats believe in social change and strong government.

Democratic National Committee - a group that provides leadership for the Democratic Party.

disaster - a sudden event that causes destruction and suffering or loss of life.

economy - the way a nation uses its money, goods, and natural resources. Economics is the science of this.

hurricane - a tropical storm with strong, circular winds, rain, thunder, and lightning.

independent - not bound by or committed to a political party.

leukemia (loo-KEE-mee-uh) - a disease characterized by an abnormal increase in white blood cells. Leukemia is a kind of cancer.

liaison (LEE-uh-zahn) - a person who establishes understanding and cooperation between groups.

liberal - favoring change and progress.

popular vote - the vote of the entire body of people with the right to vote.

Republican - a member of the Republican political party. Republicans are conservative and believe in small government.

Republican National Committee - a group that provides leadership for the Republican Party.

riot - a sometimes violent disturbance caused by a large group of people.

running mate - a candidate running for a lower-rank position on an election ticket, especially the candidate for vice president.

scandal - an action that shocks people and disgraces those connected with it.

smuggle - to import or export something secretly and often illegally.

task force - a group temporarily organized under one leader for the purpose of accomplishing a definite objective.

terrorism - the use of terror, violence, or threats to frighten people into action.

tsunami (su-NAH-mee) - a great sea wave produced by an undersea earthquake or volcanic eruption.

United Nations (UN) - a group of nations formed in 1945. Its goals are peace, human rights, security, and social and economic development.

World War II - from 1939 to 1945, fought in Europe, Asia, and Africa. Great Britain, France, the United States, the Soviet Union, and their allies were on one side. Germany, Italy, Japan, and their allies were on the other side.

WEB SITES

To learn more about George H.W. Bush, visit ABDO Publishing Company on the World Wide Web at **www.abdopublishing.com**. Web sites about George H.W. Bush are featured on our Book Links page. These links are routinely monitored and updated to provide the most current information available.

INDEX

B
Bentsen, Lloyd 17
birth 8
Bush-Overbey Oil
    Development
    Company 12
C
Carter, Jimmy 15, 16
Central Intelligence Agency
    4, 15
childhood 8, 9
Clean Air Act Amendments
    19
Clinton, Bill 24, 28
D
December 2004 tsunami
    28
Democratic Party 15, 16,
    17, 24
disaster relief 28
Dukakis, Michael 17
E
education 4, 9, 10, 11
Exxon oil spill 18
F
family 8, 9, 11, 12, 26
Ford, Gerald 15

G
George Bush Presidential
    Library and Museum
    27
Gorbachev, Mikhail 22
Gore, Al 24
H
House of Representatives,
    U.S. 4, 12, 13, 28
House Ways and Means
    Committee 13
Hussein, Saddam 20
I
inauguration 18
K
Katrina, Hurricane 28
King, Rodney 22
L
liaison to China 4, 15
Los Angeles riots 22
M
medals 4, 10
military service 4, 10, 11,
    28
Mondale, Walter 16
N
Nixon, Richard 14, 15
Noriega, Manuel 18

O
Overbey, John 12
P
Panama invasion 18
Perot, Ross 24
Persian Gulf War 4, 20, 21
Q
Quayle, Dan 17, 24
R
Reagan, Ronald 4, 16
Republican Party 4, 12, 15,
    16, 17, 24, 26
retirement 26, 28
S
Stockdale, James B. 24
Strategic Arms Reduction
    Treaty 22
U
United Nations 4, 14
United Nations ambassador
    4, 14, 28
W
Watergate scandal 15
World War II 4, 10, 28
Z
Zapata Off-Shore Company
    12
Zapata Petroleum
    Corporation 12

DISCARD